I0536532

THE

NON

CLUSIVE **X** PERIENCE

VOLUME ONE

MİSTER X

Disclaimer

What you are about to read is a work of creative expression. The events and emotions depicted within are based on my personal recollection and artistic interpretation. Names and identifying details have been changed to protect privacy.

ISBN: 979-8-9936672-1-8
The Non Xclusive Xperience
©2025 Mister X | All Rights Reserved

"For the ones who are sifting through the ashes, whispering questions into the smoke, searching for meaning among ruin…"

*"An ocean, hollowed of its years, yawns open—
I stagger through its rot, baptized in filth"*

EXORDIUM

I. ORIGO

II. LABYRINTHUS

III. INQUIETUS

IGNIRE

I. ARDOR

II. FRAGOR

III. JUDICIUM

RUINA

I. PRODITIO

II. DOLUS

III. EXCIDIUM

CINERIS

I. VESTIGIUM

II. TABES

III. INTERITUS

EXORDIUM

[eg • ZOR • dee • um]

The beginning: the introduction to a discourse.

I. ORIGO [o • REE • go]

— — — — — — — — — — — — — — — — — — — —

THE FIRST TIME

Even with our years rooted in juvenescence,

You were the verb to my subject;

The adjective to my noun;

The preposition to my phrase.

The smile that I wore

Is now the nostalgia of my days.

You were the muse of my gaze,

You were my personal Picasso,

Then time did the unthinkable—tore us apart.

Death pales in comparison.

In those few years,

You became my forever.

And while life mercilessly dragged on,

I never got the chance to show you

The legacy you carved into me:

A timeless place on the shelf of my heart.

That shelf is set apart and sacred—

It's a diamond living in a neighborhood of hatred.

Crooks and criminals plot its demise,

But it stands untouched beneath their jealous eyes,

A quiet miracle none of them can compromise.

THE TRANSITION

This foolish, immature heart ensnared,

Mourning its one true prized possession;

For this quiet grief, I was not prepared—

New lands to see, new friends, new lessons.

Some time has passed now; new connections made,

Acquaintances and even friendships, too.

But somehow it feels like a debt unpaid;

My deepest connection is still with you.

Now resentment grows from within the depths,

I must let go and start over without.

But I hesitate, consumed by doubt,

To let another walk your route.

But I try; I wander into the world,

It is here where I meet another girl.

THE POSSIBILITY

Traversing uncharted territory,

My gaze found an anchor.

Our smiles beat us to the introductions:

"Hi, my name is..."

Sparks fill the air in a blink,

Palms are sweaty.

"I'm new here..."

> *"I know. I saw you get off the bus."*

I smiled.

> *"I think we have science class together..."*

"Yeah? Can you show me where it's at?"

> *"Sure!"*

Weeks rose and fell in silence;

Nothing but stolen glances—

A smile held for just a second too long,

Sharing a secret message between us—

A message I was too afraid to read.

Then one day, her gaze shouted,

I felt it across the crowded hall.

I summoned the courage

To exchange more than mute gazes.

I approached...

"Hey!"

    "Hey!"

"Sooo, I'd like to take you out on a date, if you're up for it...?"

    "Aww...I'll think about it!"

She said, as her lips curled into a smile.

"Alright! Don't think too hard!"

I smile and walk off.

A wild drumline kicks against my ribs,

Showing the rhythm of disbelief—I did it!

A wave of pride washes over me,

Until the silence reminds me...

I have nobody to tell.

And legend has it,

She's still thinking about it..

II. LABYRINTHUS [lah • bih • RIN • thuss]

DISTRACTED

Adjust your teenage spectacles; gaze accordingly,

Into a world where change is the only constant.

A frenzied storm of what I am and who I'll be;

I'm not afraid, I'm enraged, I'm floating.

Into a world where change is the only constant,

Life and Love parallel in action.

I'm not afraid, I'm enraged, I'm floating—

I speak in a language only silence understands.

Life and Love parallel in action;

A tribe revealed, but their native tongue is foreign.

I speak in a language only silence understands,

And my tongue awakens blank stares.

A tribe revealed, but their native tongue is foreign,

But my ears echo their jokes and laughter.

And my tongue awakens blank stares;

I don't understand what's so funny.

But my ears echo their jokes and laughter;

I just want someone to ask if I want to go.

I don't understand what's so funny,

I drift in waters heavy with solitude.

I just want someone to ask if I want to go.

Discussions with myself grow more elaborate.

I drift in waters heavy with solitude.

Though I can be pretty wise, charming, and witty.

Discussions with myself grow more elaborate;

Adjust your teenage spectacles; gaze accordingly.

I can be pretty wise, charming, and witty,

In a frenzied storm of what I am, and who I'll be.

INSIDE JOB

You vanished from my sheets

To reappear at my dinner table.

A masterful sleight of hand

Performed by a familiar face

Hidden behind a borrowed heart—

A tenderness I once swore was safe.

The worst part wasn't seeing you with him.

The worst part was the math.

You knew.

He knew—he was holding the hand

I used to hold.

He smiled. You smiled.

I sat there, the only one in the room

Who didn't know the punchline.

I told the table, "We've met."

And just like that,

The gravy turned cold.

It wasn't just that you came back;

It's that you checked the guest list,

Saw my name,

And chose to walk through the door anyway.

Smiling as if our past were merely a ghost,

I felt the ground tilt beneath my feet,

And the hall closed in around me,

Caught in the quiet fury of seeing you with my own blood.

I let silence rue the awkward air…

.

SAME REFRAIN

She was an open window in a stale room

But I wasn't cool enough.

She wanted too much, too soon.

She was an open window in a stale room,

Who preferred the shadows and the gloom,

And said my edges weren't rough.

She was an open window in a stale room

But I wasn't cool enough.

ALL I WANT

—ARCHIVE: 2006—

All I want is for you to leave me be.

I don't know why you are counting on me.

I am not a machine that keeps going and going;

leave me be.

Let me be by myself

in my own little bubble

with nobody else.

Just a couple of days

to hear my thoughts clearly.

Just act like you don't know me.

Leave me be.

If I want help I'll come see you;

Don't come see me.

Just leave me be.

Teachers ask: "Is there a problem at home?"

No, the problem is here—

where you interrogate my expression.

You ask me a question

and I walk by and ignore.

Then you show up at my house,

banging on my door.

What else must I do to get you to see?

All I want

is for you to leave me be.

REFINING THE MAELSTROM [male • strum]

—I—

The road curled toward her doorway, pretending to
be hopeful,

Though every mile tasted faintly of a bruised love;

The windshield offered the night back to me, too
transparent,

As if it already knew the shape of a coming treachery.

My pulse shifted with the engine—quiet maelstrom—

Filling the car with questions in the dim interspace.

—II—

I reached her door, the night holding its breath in the
dim interspace;

I shaped my face into something steady, something
almost hopeful;

Yet the air around her porch stirred faintly, a quiet
maelstrom;

Still I knocked, pretending certainty, pretending love;

The silence inside stretched thin, a pause weighted with treachery;

And every shadow on her wall suddenly felt too transparent.

—III—

Her laptop was open, the evidence blue and transparent.

I sat at the desk, violating her interspace,

And stumbled upon the hidden line that spoke of her treachery:

"You left your panties in my bed." I had been hopeful,

But that single line assassinated our love,

And spun the room into a violent maelstrom.

—IV—

I didn't just leave; I became the maelstrom.

A shard of spite pressed in my chest, jagged and transparent.

I scorched the earth of what we called love,

Leaving nothing but smoke in the interspace.

I saw you break, and I felt no longer hopeful,

Only the grim delight of stooping to match your treachery.

—V—

I swore I'd never again be a victim of treachery.

I thought I could control the chaos, wield the maelstrom,

But looking back at the wreckage, I am far from hopeful.

My scars are visible now, ugly and transparent,

So I retreat into the safety of the interspace,

Doubting that anything whole can grow from love.

—VI—

They say forgiveness is the only cure for love,

That it washes away the stain of treachery.

But I am stranded here in the unlit skies of the interspace,

Afraid to ever again be foolishly hopeful.

I have become one with the maelstrom;

It is the only thing about me that is transparent.

—VII—

I want to believe that I can still be hopeful about love,

But the memory makes the treachery transparent.

Time in the interspace didn't heal the maelstrom, it only refined it.

III. I N Q U I E T U S [in • kwee • EH • toos]

LOVE

—ARCHIVE: 2006—

Love, love, love—

The word is unimaginative.

They say it's the greatest thing,

That you are blessed

just to be in its presence.

To feel your feet hover

in a beautiful, warm haze.

To spin in delirious circles

until it brings you to your knees,

not with worship,

but with the weight of the earth

19

and the brutal return of gravity.

You regret the encounter

with the "greatest thing."

Your head is spinning,

and suddenly, you are disgusted.

The love that once took up the space

of a thousand hearts

shrinks to a quarter-sized blemish.

And now you fill that empty space

with quiet tears,

asking the ceiling:

Will love ever love me back?

A LETTER TO MY FATHER

—ARCHIVE: 2006—

Dear Father,

I am here, speaking to you,

because I don't know what else to do.

Now that everything else has failed,

I am coming back to you.

The perfect world you wanted for us

didn't happen quite that way,

and I know this is the second time

I've knelt down here to pray.

So make an example of me

for all the world to see.

Show them the ruin of a neglected home,

how life breeds a sin all its own.

We live and we do wrong,

and the pulse of life still hurts.

I am putting my problems in your hands

so you can finally put your hands to work.

Time is passing by, you see,

and it feels like the beginning of the end.

But I know I can still count on you—

my first, my only, and my truest friend.

THE SETUP

The evening of an autumn Sunday,

worn thin by the earning of wages,

was intruded upon by a text from my mother—

unusual—

Asking me over for dinner.

The assurance of a hot meal

was a language I understood,

so I let the moment win.

The door swung open and there she was,

an exhibit in the living room,

curated by parents who made the introductions.

Then the pieces began to connect—

A shared church, a Sunday service I had missed,

their bragging whispers, all leading to this.

My father, the Saboteur of silence,

handed a folded note to her,

alleging it was my doing.

Eventually I received the same.

On it, the elementary school question:

Do you like me?

With two perfect boxes for Yes or No.

I finally realized the design of the evening,

the air in the room thick with their good intentions.

So I broke the script.

I asked if she wanted to step outside,

and it was there that hours vanished into
conversation.

We exchanged stories instead of notes,

then numbers instead of stories,

building something real from a borrowed line.

Call it an ambush of grace,

a conspiracy of hope.

The first page of the fire.

IGNIRE

[ig • NEE • reh]

To ignite: to set on fire: to burn

I. A R D O R [ar • der]

THE IGNITION

Hope dragged me reluctantly from the dark,

My old self buried in the interspace,

Hope is the matchstick; desire is the spark.

What are the chances that we make art?

I search the future for a dangerous trace,

But hope dragged me reluctantly from the dark.

I want to reciprocate, but where to start?

She reached out across the empty space,

And hope is the matchstick; desire is the spark.

I pray she carries mercy for my heart.

I try to match her steady, gentle pace,

As hope drags me reluctantly from the dark.

I asked her out to show I'll do my part.

She said yes with an easy, fluid grace,

Hope is the matchstick; desire is the spark.

I try to be optimistic—to be smart,

To break the walls I've built around my heart,

As hope dragged me reluctantly from the dark,

Hope is the matchstick; desire is the spark.

KNOCK KNOCK

I am someone who knows what I want,

But I chose to let the moment speak first.

Lest I put the cart before the hearse,

Or appear too eager, too starved, too gaunt.

Soothing my maelstrom while memories haunt,

She has gracefully twirled into my heart

Wearing daydreams of where forever starts.

I am someone who knows what I want.

Though my mind's eye is starting to focus,

The mysterious veil remains hung.

I want to be loved; a hymn unsung.

Desperation is knocking on the screen door,

Selling illusions and hocus-pocus,

Assuring myself this isn't like before.

STRIKE A MATCH

Some things happen that we struggle to forget,

But this spark has turned the dial to a dangerous heat—

A fever dormant since the Exordium.

I'm scared, but I'm burning from my head to my feet.

Lust, Love, and Desire fighting for the driver's seat.

A passionate whirlwind I don't want to lose.

But she insists this flame must remain contained;

That to express it is a right I cannot use.

I join her in the scripture's rule,

Praying for divine strength to keep the beast at bay.

But she lights the fire, she begs me to slay.

Science warns that repression makes the fool.

It turns buried desire into a volatile tool.

The pressure builds in every direction:

To architect a soul, or dismantle the connection?

I am burning at the intersection.

THE SCRIPTURE V. THE SCIENCE

—I—

At this stage of my life, I'm trying to be the most obedient.

I stand indicted by the heavens,

Charged with kidnapping my wandering thoughts

in a failed attempt to flee sexual immorality.

I have late-night phone calls with self-worth,

morning rendezvous with depression,

and I spend my evenings spooned up against rejection,

shaking hands with temptation almost hourly.

Why doesn't she want me like I want her?

—II—

Already drowning in the maelstrom, I thrash toward my work as if it were air.

Maybe if I keep my mind occupied, I won't have time to think about her.

Maybe if I work longer hours, I won't miss the touch tonight.

Maybe if my check is bigger, I can put my phone on airplane mode.

But my mind is travel-sized; it flies for free.

I'm frayed and fading, battered by this ceaseless siege.

A failed jailer, watching thoughts escape the cells I lock them in.

Now I spend my days unmoored,

spacing out into the gentler worlds of fantasy.

Why doesn't she want me like I want her?

—III—

Endless prayers plead: strengthen me, steady me, save me from myself.

I mark the church on the calendar weekly, looking for rescue.

But science foresaw the cost of this repression.

Even though each 'I love you' was true,

I donned my armor, waiting for her to yield,

While piece by piece, I vanish on this battlefield.

I carry no flag of surrender,

Only the question that haunts the defender:

Why doesn't she want me like I want her?

FEELING THE HEAT

—I—

A silent remedy to heal what haunts our home,

I have to become anonymous;

Then maybe I'll see how far my wild thoughts roam,

A silent remedy to heal what haunts our home.

Stories were shared of struggles we've all known.

We feel a shared heat scale; it is eponymous.

A silent remedy to heal what haunts our home,

I have to become anonymous.

—II—

I learned that I am not broken; there is causation.

After being anonymous for a while.

No remedy exists in a station of temptation.

I learned that I am not broken; there is causation.

Boundaries are drawn to prevent conflation,

Using career ambition to beguile.

I learned that I am not broken; there is causation.

After being anonymous for a while.

SMOLDERING INSIDE

What firepit have I fallen into?

In pursuit of the real in the unreal,

What am I meant to do?

My love's a triathlete—hydrated by gasoline;

My journey seeks one end: the welcome of her touch,

But desire is written in my cells, so I retreat to the interspace.

Walking a minefield littered with complaints,

About a career that buys everything except peace.

Frustration, Anxiety, and Depression:

Three storms vying to be the loudest,

A vortex from which I tried to hide.

But she, my heart, shall know no lack,

as long as she is mine,

Even while I am quietly unraveling.

I stepped into the buried war, wisdom invisible;

I signed a perpetual lease with my own temptation.

A tailored torment shaping the borders of my hell,

Torching the very prize I hunted.

My mood is an artist painting Insomnia.

What firepit have I fallen into?

In pursuit of the real in the unreal,

What am I meant to do?

II. F R A G O R [FRAH • gohr]

— — — — — — — — — — — — — — — — — —

AN EXPLOSION

An inconspicuous day, silently disconnected.

Complaints landing like embers

On ears congested with inadequacy.

And then—an explosion.

Adrenaline takes the moment hostage; the air grows hot.

A car door slams, shaking the stillness.

Words snarl like a cornered beast.

Another door—this time the front—slams in reply,

Sealing the storm inside.

But the hallway erupts in thunders of anguish.

"AHHHHH—WHAT DO YOU WANT FROM ME?!"

"NOTHING IS EVER GOOD ENOUGH!—"

The vase becomes a fragile comet meeting its end.

"I'M TRYING, GOD—!"

"AHHHHH!"

The keyboard meets the floor—

A another broken voice losing its letters.

Trembling hands grip my head:

"WHY CAN'T I GET THIS RIGHT?!"

"WHAT THE F—!"

A fist meets the door

In a rhythm composed by anger.

Feet heavy, each strike echoing

Like thunder in a narrow hall.

"WHAT IS WRONG WITH ME?!"

"YOU UNGRATEFUL—!"

"JUST LEAVE ME AL—!"

I dropped to my knees, drained and shaking.

Knuckles aching, ego bruised.

The living room scattered like the pieces of me.

She walks in...

THE NEW EMPLOYEE

I haven't recruited for this position before;

The demand just wasn't there.

It's not that I want you,

But I'm putting you on the payroll.

Your resume is impressive.

I am confident you'll get the job done;

You only have one task:

Take me away.

Lift me up and out of my body.

No ocean, no waves, no emotion.

Do that, and I'll label you a keeper.

A prayer I can drink to avoid my own reflection.

The job pays well, but enables something deeper.

There is peace in the missing inhibitions,

Safety in the absence of remembrance,

The denial of a real human experience.

Once you clock in for the day,

I can finally relax,

Knowing that I am safe for a little while.

THE CHAIN REACTION

A hopeful return to the ruins of nights past,

Apologies offered in search of amends,

But the embers remain awake with ire.

"I'm sorry for the damage, but not for the fire."

I'm traversing flammable ground,

Drenched in hidden accelerants.

What could go wrong?

It started with a spark—nothing more.

One careless word tossed across the kitchen floor.

Her tears couldn't extinguish these flames;

My tears failed to do the same.

I began confessing my love as if I were wearing a wire:

"I'm sorry for the damage, but not for the fire."

We can't thrive under these conditions.

"You're insufferable! Insatiable! Nothing makes you happy!"

Words thick enough to choke the truth we borrowed.

"AND YOU WILL NEVER UNDERSTAND WHAT IT'S LIKE TO BE ON THE OTHER SIDE OF YOU!"

"The other side of me?! The side that's doing everything possible to make your life easy?!"

"I NEED MORE THAN THAT! I NEED MORE FROM YOU!"

"I NEED MORE FROM YOU TOO! But boundaries, remember?!"

I stormed out before the embers could imagine cooling,

In search of a sofa to cradle what's left of me until morning.

Instead, My Employee called to offer me solace.

I let the liquid courage do what accelerants do:

Turn ache into ashes,

And memory into illusions.

THE SEPARATION

The night leaned heavy against me,

Its laughter mean and hollow.

I spent many sunsets with my New Employee,

Wishing to drown the pain in her voice

And the ire in mine.

I struggled to map her mountains of complaints

When the view looked copacetic from my seat.

Words too sharp to swallow; haunting.

Love overshadowed by the impossible,

Creating a darkness neither could ignore.

We collectively submit to the interspace,

Searching for a signal in the static we created.

No one meant to end the world that day,

But sparks don't care for meaning;

Only what is dry enough to catch.

Now there is nothing left to argue,

Only the deafening sizzle of what was once us,

Burning itself out.

III. J U D I C I U M [joo • DEE • chewma]

- - - - - - - - - - - - - - - - - - -

THE RECKONING : THE ACCELERANT

The shared excitement of this new friendship

Warms quickly, then turns strangely cold.

My intuition is working overtime,

But I refuse to clock in.

Wrapped in the haze of quality time

With my New Employee.

The ache inside me buckles,

Collapsing into mute sinkholes.

Precisely the respite I ordered.

The home I left is a threshold I can't cross again.

My words race to escape my lips,

While the air closes in—

An ambush in slow motion.

My shoulders rise, unfastened of burden;

My mind drifting somewhere far.

I catch a smile from my Employee,

With something hidden beneath the rim.

He is planting seeds of dependency,

But in this moment, none of it matters.

Just two more and maybe I'll forget my problems.

If I'm lucky, my name too.

I don't understand what else she wants me to do.

I'm already doing—

Wow, she looks amazing.

Shadows shift, and women appear from the background.

I need to get out of here.

But I feel safe; I feel like I am enough right now.

I refuse the weight of her impossible design,

The endless inventory of faults that never mend.

My Employee knows exactly what's happening.

He watches me try to douse the internal flame,

Pretending it's healing,

And not just a more flavorful way to burn.

He urges me to go back home before it's too late.

But I suspect he knows

It already is.

THE RECKONING : THE CALL

Deeply distraught, depressed, and disoriented

Silently begging for an escape from my escape.

My Employee rides shotgun; perfectly still;

Like someone who's seen this scene before.

Coherent enough to buckle up—Safety Second,

"As if you actually care about making it home,"

My Employee asserts.

Rotating the dial as I stare out into the cosmos,

Tunes ever so poignant,

Assuring me I've struck the lowest note.

I merge onto a highway to expedite my travel,

Reaching my uneventful exit

Onto the twisting surface roads.

Capped in more lines I'm sure to cross.

As my thoughts materialize,

Likewise do colorful lights in my wake.

One turn and two stop signs away from my bed,

Yet miles away from belief.

I punish the brakes beneath my foot.

I hide all of the windows at my sides,

And cautiously search for answers

To questions like: *"Have you been drinking tonight?"*

My eyes dart over to the passenger seat—eerily empty.

Absent, and yet the loudest presence in the car.

A quiet clarity rises within me:

My Employee set me up.

I step out of the car and onto a stage,

Performing for the officer,

To convince him of my regret.

"Have you ever been to jail before?"

My "NO" landed heavy on his ears,

So I turned around to accept the night's reward.

At the threshold of my weekend captivity,

I lifted the phone—then turned to stone.

Immersed in the truth.

Her number is the last lighthouse in my fogged-over mind.

Fingers trembling, breathing shallow,

I dial...the line clicks...it rings...

No one answers...

THE RECKONING : THE RELEASE

As if I had entrusted my words to a homing pigeon,

The holding cell echoed: *"You made bond!"*

My heart stuttered, my stomach tightened.

Tired, cold, and hungover,

I stumble in the officer's wake.

Words fill the airwaves,

But every sound slips through.

At a desk, his fingertip sketches the invisible,

And I—ink-bound—hurry after.

He points at the door and nods.

I exhale...

I step through that door

and someone hands me a slip.

Something about a court date ran across her lips.

"Here are your belongings."

"Where is my wallet?"

"You didn't have one when you came in, sir."

My mind aghast.

Just another notch on the belt of things to fix.

My shameful, anxiety-ridden eyes focus on the exit,

Where the rusted gates complained as they opened.

I emerged from the shadows, and there she was.

I saw relief in her eyes, but annoyance all over.

She offered a tight-lipped inquiry:

"Are you okay?"

"Yeah, I'm fine. It's been an interesting night.

Let's get out of here before they change their mind."

Our exchanges reached a bare minimum.

It was painfully obvious she didn't want to be here.

Even her silence had somewhere better to be.

THE RECKONING : THE VERDICT

I know life has been the altar of my ambitions, but I never

Meant for us to be the sacrifice.

Sometimes I really can't tell if you love me,

Or if I'm simply exasperation that you endure, but the

Reality is we're both seeking the same shore, both

Reaching for solid ground, a permanence to trust for

Years to come.

I love you; all the constellations in my sky spell your name

Let's trust our love—move away from toxic fumes, I would

Love for that to be all that mattered right now, but the

D.A. wanted to throw the book at me so I made some calls.

Only the first offense...

But I still have to do a little time, and after that, I promise

Everything is going to be fine.

Tell me that you still love me...

This doubt is worse than any reality I've found myself living

Even if you won't allow your lips to reveal that secret,

Remember why you have that secret to tell in the first place.

THE RECKONING : THE INTAKE

I absorbed your words, each one like a bruise that still remembers and

Forgiveness doesn't come easy, but love was never meant to be easy either.

Our altar cracked, yet I still trace its edges with onus, not blame.

Regret, I've learned, is just another form of longing and

Guilt has made ghosts of us both—let's dwell among them no more.

Inside your storm, I still saw the man who built dreams, not ruins.

Vows don't vanish; they echo until we choose to answer them and

Even the time you'll serve can't sentence my heart to silence.

You ask if I still love you—yes, in the quiet way a scar remembers the wound.

Our story is imperfect, but it's ours; I'd rather rebuild than erase;

Until you're free, I'll keep the light on—so you'll know where home is.

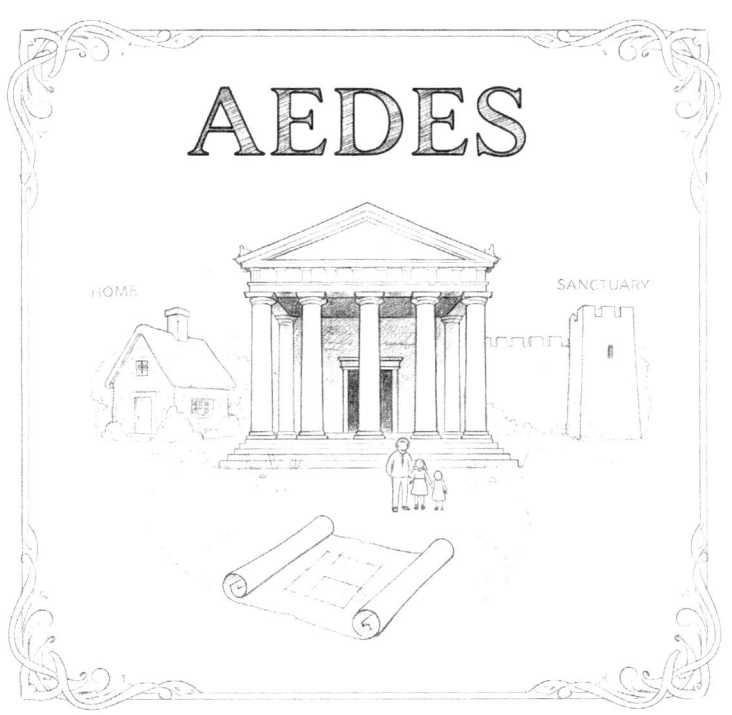

AEDES

HOME   SANCTUARY

[ah • E • des]

Sanctuary: Home

I. FUNDAMENTUM [foon • dah • MEN • toom]

— — — — — — — — — — — — — — — — — —

THE ARCHITECT

I am the contact you keep on speed dial,

The one called to survey the ruins

Smoldering on this scorched earth.

I am here to answer if love can be cultivated

In this soil dressed in ash.

I spend days in my office scouring the schematics of us,

Conceiving the most durable restorative material.

My budget mirrors the horizon of the wreckage,

And this is not the hour to count costs.

Lest I revel in watching love depart—

For it evidently demands an audience—

I must certify my intention:

I am not building for beauty,

But for survival.

Or perhaps, I won't build at all.

Instead, I'll listen to what the walls remember.

I'll even accept that some ruins

Prefer to stay that way.

But if the walls hold,

And once love has been rebuilt,

We'll conduct the post-occupancy evaluation.

Together.

CLEARING THE RUBBLE

We labour as the days rise and fall prey,

We witness the dust and smog following.

We see with clarity granted today,

The uncertainties of love—hollowing;

Brick after brick laid perfectly to rest,

Resent is not a mint worth swallowing,

Nor a scattered heap I cannot refresh.

So we formed a bond in a stateroom

Reinforced by steel attestations' mesh

Of a love bearing weight unlike a plume,

Though our love triumphs in destruction's wake,

We falter to celebrate our loves rune.

Until assuredness breathes beside our ache,

We're walking, still, on fragile beams that quake.

THE STATEROOM

Imagine walking a mile in my hidden tomb,

Where hope and doubt entwine and bloom,

"You all can come on back now, into my stateroom."

Atmosphere uncharted, discomfort thick in the air

> *"Hi, I'm Doctor—"*

I nervously shift in my chair;

> *"Tell me a little bit about what brings you two in today..."*

She says, *"A lot of issues with communication, and he's been dealing with some anger issues, and depression, and it's caused a lot of pain."*

My defeated silence is screaming as our eyes connect...

> *"...and what about you, what's troubling you Mister X?"*

I see a small window laden with opportunity;

A chance to speak, to gather scattered hearts.

Doubtful, I lift my voice and let each word carry its own weight...

"Well, Doc, I'm just tired;

And I don't mean like I need a nap tired,

I mean—soul tired, heart too heavy to lift tired.

I love her...God, I love her more than anything,

But my brain is wired for a kind of closeness

We're not allowed to share.

And that gap—that distance—it eats at me everyday.

Working hard to provide, but starving to be held.

So I build my distance,

So that every touch doesn't feel like another ride

On a rollercoaster I didn't agree to get on.

And when she looks at me, puzzled by the space I've made,

I quietly swallow the anger and let it melt into sadness,

And call it fatigue—

Until the word becomes true.

Then I reconnect with My Employee

Sharing a co-worker's kindness, a laugh in the hallway—

Reminding me of what it feels like to be enough,

And I hate myself for needing that reminder.

Because home—home is so full of complaints

I can barely fit through the door.

At night, I climb into bed beside her bare flesh,

Nothing between us but the silence of dreams—

And turn the other cheek.

Betrayed by sleep, I rise and bury my weary mind

In the only thing that will have me—work.

And in the kind of lonely, private moments

I don't talk about—

Moments that make me feel both human for a second,

And pathetic right after—

Just to survive another sunrise; and the cycle repeats."

An awkward pause grabs the clock;

The time is kept only through the pounding of my heart

"Wow, that's a lo—you've got a lot going on there...and you two are...not married, correct?"

"Correct!"

The compass starts here and the work—

No longer just words.

Our destination is distant.

May our feet fall in rhythm.

II. S A N C T U M [sangk • tuhm]

THE BLUEPRINT

A thought born from the stateroom's repetition

A shared, majestic vision of an Aedes,

A place to harbor both a bride and groom,

Despite a love that feels almost ascetic.

The question of "how many?" felt almost moot.

She said *"I want three"*, and I said, "Just one",

And so we compromised and landed at "Two"

She was so hopeful for a daughter; I, a son.

A full house, then. I thought, "That should be fun."

"But I want to stay home for the first year."

I said, "A mother's job is never done."

I'll do what fathers do: rock the baby, sip some beer.

I knew it when I said it. She only heard "some beer".

This is the line we drew: no drinking around the child

A bad example was her deepest, truest fear.

I knew I'd have to tread carefully, lest she revile.

"We'll need more space—each child should have a room"

(Though what toddler guards borders?)

The idea felt years too early, too soon—

But the photographs demanded their perfect order.

Her lips curled into a smile, delighted by the name—

A thing I'd barely spared a thought—

"If it's a girl you choose, the boy is mine to claim".

Then she proudly laid out everything she'd bought.

We glowed together at the future taking shape;

Perfection waits for no one—we'd be waiting forever

We knew the choice was heavy, no easy escape,

Yet vowed that time would never steal our endeavor.

SPONSALIA [spohn • SAH • lee • ah] [Engagement]

We share a bountiful love forged in flame,

So fierce a candle's glow might burn in envy.

Your smile, a force that rises up to mend me

Now a vibrant spark; it deserves a name

Call it endless—we started infinity,

Assured no mortal end could pull apart.

Call it distinguished—our star for eternity,

A compass drawn within each other's heart.

These distant voices fade, become obscure,

A trembling voice prepares what fate decreed.

My courage gathers, steady yet unsure—

The moment blooms; it's time to plant the seed.

Both hands entwined, I fall to bended knee:

Beloved—will you marry me?

NUPTIALS [Wedding]

I vow to love and lead you all my life,

My partner, equal, and my dearest friend,

To cherish and support you as my wife,

A sacred bond that even death cannot transcend,

A union that we vow now to defend,

With joyful memories to feed its flame,

And pledge to you the honor of my name.

THE THRESHOLD

My body reached for what our vows allowed,

A cabin suite, to fan the dying embers.

The ocean's voice was heavy, deep, and loud,

Weeping a pain that only she remembers.

A cabin suite, to fan the dying embers.

Blindly groping as the moment passes,

Weeping a pain that only she remembers.

Distorting sweet honey to bitter molasses.

Blindly groping as the moment passes,

Trapped inside a cruel and cold illusion,

Distorting sweet honey to bitter molasses

Docile streams now torrential rivers of confusion.

Trapped inside a cruel and cold illusion,

No rescue workers on duty today,

Docile streams now torrential rivers of confusion;

I toss a buoy but watch it float away,

No rescue workers on duty today,

A cabin suite, to fan the dying embers.

I toss a buoy but watch it float away,

Weeping a pain that only she remembers.

III. F I S S U R A [fis • shu • ra]

THE MAELSTROM'S ECHO

Is it rejection or is it trauma's work?

Don't pull the thread of a stitched-up wound.

My trauma watches with a knowing smirk.

Is it rejection or is it trauma's work?

"She doesn't want you—of course it hurts!"

"Hush! Think about it—maybe it's just too soon."

Is it rejection or is it trauma's work?

Don't pull the thread of a stitched-up wound.

THE SECRETUM [Secret]

I found myself living a duality I never wanted,

A split existence that eventually haunted.

It came with validation I needed, but wasn't seeking,

Acknowledgement that fed me, but I wasn't keeping.

I only wanted my beloved's reverence,

But lost the road, searching ever since.

My 'husband' title feels like a defeat,

My 'colleague' title feels like a reprieve.

At home, I'm distant; I simply do not care,

To them, a man who tries is distinct and rare.

At home, I'm guarded, I can't be bothered,

To them, I'm a seed that simply needs water.

At home, I'm obsessive, it fills the house with doubt;

To them, it's the certainty their partners live without.

At home, I offer no praise or concessions,

To them, a wife should want that deep obsession.

At home, I'm moody, often aggressive,

To them, it's a reaction to the repressive.

At home, I'm just a visitor, a ghost within the fable,

To them, I am a man with a seat at the table.

I weathered the storm, though I was beset,

They didn't make it across, never really a threat.

I refocused my heart to where it was needed,

My subdued critiques were finally loud enough to be heeded.

GRAVIDA [Heavy; Pregnant]

Today beheld a gift bereft of calm,

A heavy silence, thick within the pew.

The pain above reproach without a balm,

My one belov'd colludes with the prie-dieu.

I loosed the cord and gave my world to you;

Then heaven bent to warm thy visage mild,

And in thy cry, eternity reconciled.

THE NURSERY

We've built this place for your small head to rest,

I built the crib and tightened every screw;

Your mommy picked the blanket—only the best,

And I picked out this cute and tiny shoe.

I'm awkwardly holding you, I'm still learning,

Mommy promised it gets easier with time.

Every burp, every cry, is ever concerning,

Until you laugh, and everything is fine.

I rest you on my chest and tap your little nose,

Your sudden laughter melts away my stress;

And when I tickle your little toes,

In those moments, I feel like a success.

Daddy doesn't know just what to do when you cry,

I'll get it wrong, and start all over again;

But never for a second think that I won't try,

It'll always be your little heart I seek to win.

RUINA

COLLAPSE

DESTRUCTION

DESTRUCTION

[roo • EE • nah]

Ruin: Collapse

I. PRODITIO [proh • DEE • tee • oh]

— — — — — — — — — — — — — — — — — — —

THE BASIUM [BAH • see • um] [Kiss]

As if I'd crossed the path of karma's law,
It tracked the breadcrumbs of the maelstrom's end
To serve me humble pie, and serve it raw.
I'd sooner spit and throw it in the bin.

My starving ears devoured every word,
Leaving my gut hollow, sick, and stirred.

"I was in a dark place and he was there"

He took my seat, and ordered from my chair.

"It only happened once, and I was going to—"

As if betrayal earns a slot on the calendar.
Silently aghast, I'm swallowing my sword;
Reaping, reaping, reaping all at once,

A truth to which I humbly acquiesce,
But still, the inner wound remains untouched,
So does the burning question, "Is it really mine?",

No context stops the bleeding or the mess,
Of a tender wound kept wet by cruel reminders.

For that reality, I am equipped.

My Employee has earned a phone call.

THE PERFORMANCE REVIEW

Let's take a moment to speak,
though it may be fleeting,
A crowded calendar commands my clock;
This quarter's results
show where I'm taking a beating.

We've worked together on projects before:
"The Explosion," "The Intake," "The Call"—
Each one with an audit finding we cannot ignore.

Let's log these as opportunities for improvement;
I see potential to reverse this losing trend,
It's your trademark: this reckless, destructive
movement.

But there are some key metrics where you excel:
Your support on 'Swallowing the Sword' is noted,
You help to numb the protest I can never tell.

I must admit that the feedback was all true,
You really are the best at what you do,
Let's move to agenda Line Item number two.

My spreadsheet of problems shows a deficit of hope;
This is now your top priority task,
The business needs your expertise on how to cope.

So go ahead and take your bow,
Your performance delivers on its reputation.
The numbing is my need, and I need it now.

THE TRESPASSER

I heed the counsel of the whispered voice within,
A hallowed murmur at the third eye's gate.
The command came, a blank and sudden chill,
And so I obliged, the "why" a mist.

I heed the counsel of the whispered voice within.

The turning wheels unwound the tangled "why,"
The engine cooled, and clarity arrived.
A threshold crossed by a forbidden guest;
Panicked thoughts rushing to one conclusion.

My feet met the pavement, my gaze met his;
Our faces worlds apart in what they held.
No syllables wasted but malice filled the air.
One foot inside and—
My home read to me a story my mind rejected.

I heed the counsel of the whispered voice within.

It screams the messenger betrayed the errand,
The air replete with evidence; a punishing truth.
My throat grew raw, lashing out with a violent tongue,
My grief, now a spectacle verified by stares.

"THE AUDACITY YOU—"

My implosion writing a new narrative,

The self I was, erased in disarray;

"LEAVE!"
—My intuition almost equally aggressive.
I heed the counsel of the whispered voice within.

My daughter strapped safely, as everything else
broke loose,
I race in pursuit of the bleak horizon.
My only rescue, bound in numbers and a prayer.
From the collapsing ledge of my own mind

I only brought two small offerings to the aftermath:
Silence...and Absence.

I heed the counsel of the whispered voice within.

II. D O L U S [do • luss]

– – – – – – – – – – – – – – – – – – – –

ULTIMATA [ool • tee • mah • tah]

There are moments in love
So steeped in self-deception,
You can taste the lie on your tongue.
This is one of mine.

My devotion to fighting for love
Has left me blind.
If I could see,
I'd name this for what it truly is—
But truth, for me, is still a foreign language.

I want to believe there's love left to mend.
I don't want to believe I am the wound,
Though I may very well be.

And I can't yet accept
That my exalted wife—
The saint I've built from memory and need—
Is capable of such quiet betrayals.

So I return, contempt heavy in my chest,
And force my lips to play the part.
"I'm back, but he has to go away.
I've said it before, and I stand by the demand:

You get me or you get him. But not both."

You say nothing...
And in that silence, I hear the verdict.
Empty moments fill the distance between us.
*"He's a really good friend, he adds value to my life.
I think you're overreacting."*

As I stand before the wreckage of us,
Offering everything I am,
While you weigh our history
Against his friendship.
You hold the scale—
And I, the sentence.

I watch you, amazed,
how your silence sharpens into defense
Instead of the clean slice of truth
I ache for.

It's strange—
how the smallest details
align to answer the largest questions,
whispering their cruel certainties.

Why am I still fighting for this,
When it's clear I am not enough?

Somewhere in my own deception,
I lie again—
And call it hope.

THE PROMOTION

Thank you for joining me, albeit last minute,
This meeting is defined by your presence.
Our scheduled syncs have reached their limit,
So let's get straight to the essence.

A higher rung is now within your grasp,
Your name was the first thought it invoked.
Your primary focus? To do as you're asked,
And suppress the fire that has lately smoked.

We spoke before on where your skills could grow,
Untapped potential, and findings from the audit.
Now the business needs a third party to show
How to stop the bleeding of our profit.

They need to demo products, in hopes that we buy-in,
And transform our processes to meet business needs.
The market is tough, the margins are thin,
And the red on the ledger spreads like weeds.

To put it quite plain, the terms have changed,
It's starting to feel like a hostile takeover.
It feels my very borders are being re-arranged,
And this is the moment that defines your makeover.

I need you to execute, and without fail,
Mask the signs of this hostile takeover.
Your arsenal of pilsners and ales is stale,

And won't serve for what the task now entails.

You'll have your choice of a few different hats,
I'll gladly submerge in your sparks of ingenuity.
Bourbon, Whiskey, heck, even Cognac,
To ensure our operational continuity.

Moonshine and Tequila are on the list, too,
I'll cover for you until the break of dawn.
I'll sign off on whatever means you pursue,
Just make this go away... before you're gone.

THE FULL HOUSE

A space within the hearth was never filled,
A love now bound by blood and by bequest.
A joy a father only knows to share,
I saw my bond cemented in those eyes.

My sweet, sweet son, my life begins again;
You have my eyes, my ears, my innocent heart.
I cannot shield you from the whole world's harm,
But you are safe when wrapped within my arms.

My son, you're here with family, know this well:
Show all respect, but never let truth be blind.
The truth demands your work, there is no easy way;
Life cares not for your feelings, but your deeds.

My solemn vow is to provide a home.
I wish for you to know what makes a man:
It is not measured by the wealth you bring.
The world is cold; let wisdom be your coat.

If I teach you nothing else in this life:
That wit and strength are naught, if truth is lost.
Stand for beliefs, though you may stand alone.

When you can grasp the meaning of my words,
Know that while I stand, I stand with you.
My sweet, sweet son.

FOOLISH CONCESSIONS

Time has grown another year older,
While resonance refuses to mature.
His name, a constant rhythm on her tongue;

"I miss my friend", she says, and the words stab
slowly.

I thought myself brave for loving a storm,
But I was only ever touched by the lightning.

If he is the reason for her easy smile,
Perhaps my chance has not yet died in vain.
I'll learn my rival's art, and in a while,
Re-learn the way to make her smile again.

I allowed the severed tether to be re-tied;
(He is forbidden from the Aedes' gate).
But I witnessed joy she could not hide—
A silent dagger, sealing up my fate.

I called my ruin "devotion,"
And wore my folly like a crown of faith.
The fool in me mistook the wound for warmth,
And called the bleeding proof of my love.

I was the fool who called my chains allegiance,
The dreamer who mistook the cliff for sky.

The Jester's crown adorns me now.

THE DUX [Leader]

The calendar turned a dozen months more,
But the script stayed the same.
The residue of my delusion stains;
The dagger I met while making concessions remains.

My gaze grew sharp, competing with the hawk:
Random smiles, sudden app changes, skittish replies.
Each moment silently archived—
Am I paranoid, or is this where trust dies?

I stayed aloof through every stage of "I told you so,"
Days fermenting to weeks—the phone a guarded
gate.

We circled the same futile arguments,

While I watched others get what I still beg for.
I felt like the variable
that kept breaking the equation,
Trying to function with null values—
it all felt undefined.

I stepped out to check the mail,
But my eye caught the flash of a name on the screen.
The laughter's source... now crystal clear.

I ousted the clandestine phone from the pillow,
Opened it—confirmed what I already suspected.

Message after message of his begging—
And she co-signs the tease, so long as he stays cool.

Insomnia wins another night—storms of maelstrom.
I retreated into the darkness of sleepless slumber, sick,

Seeking comfort from the cold side of the pillow,
Wrapped in a blanket of confirmation.

By noon I was bound for a hotel stay with My Employee.

Frantically retracing ruins, digging up bones,
Asking questions, reliving the arguments,
In a chokehold by the echo.

Am I that awful? Have I built a prison or an Aedes?
My heart was true, but trust betrayed me.
When the moment demanded integrity, some faltered.

But this is my family—sitting at the high-stakes table.
So I changed uniforms to become the Pit-boss.

This is my delusion:
choosing the new lie of a better road.
I'm fighting for a home that gave up fighting for me.

THE DISCOVERY

Clocks melted into evenings, and evenings into
dreams,
I'm drifting,
Through the peaceful realms of nightfall,
Disarmed...
Vulnerable.

An idle mind,
Suddenly carved with curiosity,
Cats, beware

A trembling voice confirmed what she'd unearthed;
Each syllable quivered, half accusation, half hurt.

The Secretum, buried years ago, resuscitated—
Climbing from the shallow grave to feed upon my
dreams.

A nudge, growing with conviction.
        "I can't believe you, what is this?"

She shoves the phone in my face.
"What is what?" I said.

My eyes recoiling from the sharp white light.
        "You said I was lazy! I can't—"

"What? What are you talking about?"

Midnight wasn't far behind;
I grabbed the phone and began to read...
My memory jogs, then stalls in sudden dread;
Confounded at these messages
I had left for dead years ago.

Confident they had reached their grave—
Yet... here we are.

"You don't have anything to say?"

I...do.
I'm just...
Confused...

I don't know why these ghosts are haunting my
phone.

"Well..."

"Ok, I'm sorry. Let me start there..."

"I'm sorry...for hurting you, and how you found out."

"Those messages are just relics from the past,
From a time when I was truly alone.
When our love felt the most hollow and unsound,
I had no one left to speak to.
Every conversation ended with a 'fix' for me,
And never with an ear for my reality.
I went searching for solace on a different ground,

I lamented the ache, the rust, the rot,
In hopes they held some wisdom you did not.
In your expression, I can see the sting of the rust,
My intention wasn't to hurt you, it was to help us.

The circumstances planted a desperate seed,
My words at the time were inappropriate—a frantic plea.

When we're at war, I have no one, not a soul.
The emptiness consumes me, taking its toll.

But my intention isn't what I'm on trial for—
I hurt you, and I'm sorry..."

"I need some time to think."

"I understand..."

THE OPEN DOOR

The wheel of a dozen months groans a second time;
Our hearts existing in a deep, unspoken sigh,
Yet mine still holds a cadence of resistance.

A conversation born of dejected desperation;
A once vibrant soul, now decrepit and dilapidated,

Gasping for air in what was once an ocean of
affection,
Now an unruly pool of algae, blood, and sludge.

*"I love you, but I'm miserable—I have been for
a while now."*

Your silent grief is etched into a gaze of disdain.
I have poured my last drop, and yet your cup is
raised.

*"But my needs are very specific; I can't really
explain."*

And yet you assert that these words
must be expedited?

I no longer know what I am offering—
My heart keeps reaching but never finds a warm
reception.

"I know it's not really the best timing, but I'm drowning,"

"Drowning?! In the pool I built for you to rest in? Just. Stand. Up."

"I just need a distraction for a little bit, this is all too much."

"Too much?!
I turn left, and you condemn the path.
I turn right, and you condemn the pace.
I turn flips, and you condemn the form.
And you are the one...who finds this too much?"

"No! That's not the answer; it won't heal your pain."

As I think to myself:
What new hell can we possibly attain?

"The mending of our marriage demands our attention!"

"You're not wrong, but what do you suggest? How do we fix it?"

"I don't have the answer or the ending, but I'm certain this isn't it!"

"I really need a distraction right now, just for a little bit..."—as she weeps gently

"Do you feel this deeply—now, of all times?!

Look at me, look into my eyes and tell me:
This chaos is what you call need?"

*"It is, I'm suffering and I'm trying to do it
quietly but I need a distraction."*

I let silence interject,
As I took my seat in thought...

Through the long corridor of years;
Doing emotional gymnastics
To keep the show alive,

Now you tell me you need a break
From watching me perform?

As if it's harder to watch the circus
Than to be the one breaking bones for the applause.

How do I call this prison a home?
The light within flickers like our love; like our
marriage.

"You're really begging your husband for—"
I shake my head,
Devoid of expression and defeated.

My babies deserve a world
Where home means mommy and daddy together.
But how much longer can I sit in this burning house

And inhale the smoke?

Knowing each grief-stricken breath
Steals a little more of the husband I want to be?

Knowing even if I stand firm,
The spine of "us" is already fracturing…
Will I hear it finally snap?

I dominate the silence with one phrase…

"…Fine. It won't heal anything,
Only speed up the unraveling our eyes have
witnessed in slow motion."

III. E X C I D I U M [ecks · CHEE · dee · um]

RUSHES

The circle of a year,

And a heavy sorrow more,

Has bloomed and withered again.

That "Open Door" breathed an unbearable breeze,

Letting in more biting things than healing winds,

As wisdom assured me.

That door slammed shut quickly with a purposeful
ferocity,

To attempt restoration of a ruin in progress.

I heed the counsel of the whispered voice within.

Even with eyes wide shut, exploring other realms,

The whispers carry like a fresh aroma through the air;

Interdimensional enticement holds a certain weight.

Weeks ago, security measures taken for protection.

Sharp words no longer the only weapon that dwells

In the midst of a silence honed to kill;

But the blood in the silence is the only truth that tells.

I heed the counsel of the whispered voice within.

Startled in a cold sweat, heart doing jumping jacks,

Awakened to what was no longer a whisper—

As if my intuition climbed into bed to be the big spoon.

And so I obliged, the "why" still a mist.

Through the camera's cold, dilated pupils,

I saw the moment that lit a fuse inside.

The camera didn't blink, but I did—to clear the tears...

As the fractured spine finally snapped.

I can't...

Enough—

I don't understand. I can't win. F...

(*sigh*)

Somehow, I rolled over...and went to sleep.

The later confrontation: a soft rehearsal of lies.

"It's not what you think"

A lie as tired as I, from a restless slumber.

Words escape me as grief and anger bubble over.

My hands have never been so eager.

"I'm going to take a drive."

I heed the counsel of the whispered voice within.

Accompanied by the sound of rubber kissing cement,

Striking the dashboard, tempting the airbags,

Screams that only the window-fog could witness.

My name carved in this pain before; I won't sign it again.

I return composed, with a single phrase to offer:

"We need to start discussing this divorce arrangement."

THE SOUL CRY

Mine eyes have given way to beautiful tears before,

Ones that could rival The Starry Night.

But never has sorrow's tide within

Surged beyond its perimeter.

'til now...

I was a proud man—until the wind of truth gave me chills.

Proud of the Aedes built from scratch,

Proud of my beautiful babies, that chapter complete,

Proud of my provisions—the table always full.

But now...

I stand amid the flames that accompany my pride.

Whiskey in hand, I let it warm my insides,

While I settle on the bed's edge, awaiting her shadow.

When she comes, our words are brief, then sharp.

I tell her: "Don't bring him near my babies."

She deflects again; *Is that a threat?"*

Eyes deadpan; I sip my drink.

The talk turns toward that night we shouldn't
mention— When touch became another wound.

She says,

    "You did me a favor by filing for this divorce."

Silence interrupts...

Stunned. Slack-jawed and wide-eyed...

I whispered to the ghost of us,

"I only did what you told me to do."

She collected a few items and stormed off to her
room.

I remained seated, finishing my drink,

While fury boiled beneath my skin.

I crushed my cup. Adrenaline surged.

My body's burning,

Hands trembling,

Lip quivering,

Eyes watering...

GO!

I heed the counsel of the whispered voice within.

This was not a fire drill;

The bomb threat is imminent.

Every step urgent,

I race to my office where the alcohol awaits.

My urgency warranted attention; she stalked my footsteps,

Her voice only grazed my ear—all sound, but no sense.

At last, my office—

I manhandle the strongest bottle.

It spills, drenching my shirt...

The mess matching the storm inside.

I wiped my stache and began my trek to a quiet place.

Being stingy with my syllables,

I make my way through the kitchen to the hallway,

Before she becomes a blockade in my path.

I can't touch...

I can't talk...

Handicapped with rage—I dropped to my knees...

A wail escapes my body;

A bawl unlike anything I knew I was capable of.

A caterwaul from the depths of my soul...

Gutted...undone...grief-stricken...

For love...

As the scream decayed, her voice pierced the quiet:

"I'm sorry, I didn't mean it."

My tears weren't done watering my grave.

A piece of me died on that floor;

Vexed it wasn't the whole of me.

A man emptied by his own devotion.

I rise and continue my trek.

I kiss the kids goodnight before retiring to my bed,

Waiting to pass out

From a job well done by My Employee.

Before I knew it, I was burdened by the sunrise,

Showing the ghost of warmth in an unmade bed.

Again, the pillow catches every drop of my anguish.

Now I weep for the man that I couldn't be.

Despite it all, clandestine beneath the torment,

Love continued its residence;

The same address where my self-hate was born.

I gave every morsel of myself to a ravenous flame,

Now I am left just a trembling ember...

THE HOSTILE TAKEOVER

To: All Faculties

From: The New Management

Date: Effective Immediately

Subject: Corporate Restructuring

and Change in Leadership

I came not to barter, but to brandish—

Your empire now folds into mine.

Your leader—formally, and permanently—

Unburdened of his charge.

Your boardroom fell like kingdoms do…

Quietly, then together in time.

His "Promotion" and "Performance Review"

Both kind yet asinine,

Our new policy: "Foolish Concessions" are assets we
now decline.

I came not to barter, but to brandish—

Your empire now folds into mine.

Love—an acquisition he chased through spreadsheet lines,

He failed to see the ledger bleeding out the warning signs.

Your boardroom fell like kingdoms do...

Quietly, then together in time.

I will "demo" a love forged

In my "rudimentary arsenal's" shrine,

The "top priority task" is changed to mandatory overtime.

I came not to barter, but to brandish—

Your empire now folds into mine.

Let us define the horizon of the "Blueprint"

before we draw the line,

Coping and survival act as passengers to the design.

Your boardroom fell like kingdoms do...

Quietly, then together in time.

Welcome to the new "Aedes"—financed by your

Lead Investor's spine.

The "Employee" is now the CEO;

The papers are ready to sign.

I came not to barter, but to brandish—

Your empire now folds into mine.

Your boardroom fell like kingdoms do...

Quietly, then together in time.

THE POSTMORTEM

The Aedes, a joint shelter at the start of this long
defeat.

But the gall of those late-night revelries—

A poison I couldn't stomach,

While I kept a lonely vigil of our young.

Exiled into the arms of family;

The Aedes staged for sale; a casualty in tandem.

Its ruin ignored, I cross the town to address the filth,

Concealing the betrayal, bound in paper.

I arrive at her cold haven—the guest room.

The source of my own winter—

Now the narrator of my anguish.

The "why" had grown too frantic to ignore,

The question was a sickness in my head.

I let my eyes drink the words that nearly struck me dead:

"...more words linger—patient, waiting for the right moment with you..."

No time for my mind to brace for impact.

I've been begging for all of you, I'm confused.

"...there was a moment when familiar arms tugged at me again, a warmth I used to know, but I stood still, and the disappointment showed..."

My breath catches—I know those arms. I know that failure.

"...I spoke of how you've become the one I reach for. When asked if you were the one, the yes came as naturally as breathing..."

I fold, fragmented at the nearest bin.

My stomach, now at war, retches the truth I just swallowed.

I re-count the times I begged for confessions:

Is there another? Are you untrue?

I reproduce the denials that sealed my worthlessness.

Unnamed parts of her heart were bolted shut; only to me.

Her insistence that the Door remained closed

Was the lie that kept me blind,

Though I felt the tremors beneath the words,

Revealing the hierarchy of ghosts now:

The 'Trespasser' was the war I thought I'd already fought.

'Rushes' was but a clever, noisy decoy to draw my fire.

His presence merely smoke…

Masking the true flame burning within the pages.

I recall the ferocity of that Door slamming shut—

Merely a show to appease—The latch never caught;

The heist was an inside job—

A specter, burdened with a heartbeat.

All this chaos and haze—

A stage for the flame of which her heart bowed to,

While I stood outside its warmth.

For me? She spoke the line that broke my world:

> *"I was never going to leave you."*

The "Ruina" is complete.

CINERIS

ASHES

REMINANTS

EMBERS

TEBS OET

REBIRTH

[kee • NAIR • iss]

Ashes

DISCLAIMER

A note to the Reader,

The final section of this collection, Cineris, is a raw and honest exploration of the ashes. It contains unfiltered depictions of severe depression, anxiety, substance abuse, and suicidal ideation.

If you are sitting in your own ashes and find your story in these, please know that you are not alone. You can reach the National Suicide & Crisis Lifeline by calling or texting

988

This story is one man's, but the experience is "Non-Xclusive"

I. VESTIGIUM [ves · TEEJ · ee · um]

CAPTIVUS TURBINIS [Prisoner of the Storm]

Trapped in a tireless rainsquall, mind astir,
The fresh tearing-open of what barely held.
"But you were never going to leave me..."
How long have I danced in circles,
Mistaking them for paths?

The fresh tearing-open of what barely held;
I forged a man to make it through the dark,
But I was never your kind of light.
How long have I danced in circles,
Mistaking them for paths?

I forged a man to make it through the dark,
I must be fucking delusional.
But I was never your kind of light.
"But you said you loved me!"

I must be fucking delusional.
What the hell is wrong with me!
"But you said you loved me!"
Why even parade my surname?

What the hell is wrong with me!
And our family's fragile flame?
Why even parade my surname?

I hope his arms are worth the ruin.

And our family's fragile flame?
My beloved sees only the space where I vanish.
I hope his arms are worth the ruin.
You were the axis on which my small world turned.

My beloved sees only the space where I vanish;
I faltered at the altar of my biggest resolve.
You were the axis on which my small world turned.
But my broken self broke more than just me.

I faltered at the altar of my biggest resolve;
I sought only truth, to heal us.
But my broken self broke more than just me.
I could not grovel; I was made to stand tall.

I sought only truth, to heal us;
I hold a lie called possibility—a hollow thing.
I could not grovel; I was made to stand tall.
Now I drink to forget, but never forget to drink.

I hold a lie called possibility—a hollow thing.
Trapped in a tireless rainsquall, mind astir.
Now I drink to forget, but never forget to drink.
The fresh tearing-open of what barely held.

ANXIETY

No air
No air
Walls—
Closer—
Closer still—

Heartbeat Heartbeat Heartbeat

Sinkhole
In chest
No bottom

Hands shake
Mouth dry
Eyes burn
Skin crawls

Ring off
Skin pale
The mark remains:
Ghost circle,
Still warm

Papers signed
But not done
Never done
Nothing done
Not enough

Coffee, cold
Again
Again
Stomach twists
Like rope
Tightens—tighter
Tighter still

Heartbeat Heartbeat Heartbeat

Phone Buzzes
Don't look
Look anyway
Empty screen
No name
No sound

The clock
Won't move
Won't stop

Breath caught
In ribs
Can't get out.
Can't get out.
Can't get—

Pulse loud
Ears filled
White noise
Inside my skull
I'm shrinking

Inside
Myself
A crawlspace
A furnace
A cage
Heartbeat Heartbeat Heartbeat
Light hurts
Shadows crowd
World shakes
Too close
Too sharp
Too loud.

Love
Gone
Self
Gone

Heartbeat Heartbeat Heartbeat

No air
No air
Help.

DISSOCIATION

I sit in my office
Work is the focus
The light is warm
The clock is slow
Think: sloth

*"You'll never know what it's like being on the other
side of you—"*

The vent clangs,
I feel the heat,
I hear the growl.
Breakfast is calling.
And my coffee is on hold.

*"—you did me a favor by filing for this damn
divorce—"*

The mug is burning my hand.
Too heavy
Then too light.
I lift it
And miss my mouth.

"Is that a threat?—"

I'm pacing the room.
I'm sitting.

I haven't moved
In hours,
I think.

"—I don't care what you do in those streets, keep that
shit away from my babies!"

The chair creaks.
Or maybe that was me.
Arthritis hurts.
I can't feel my arm.
Everything hums.

"—The audacity you have to disrespect me in my
house by bringing his stuff here."

Oh, an hour passed.
I need to login
The shades are shut.
I watch them breathe.

"—Put the damn phone down, I'm trying to have a
conversation with you—"

Am I?
The words slip out, heavy with contempt.
The moment hangs there.
Like smoke
That doesn't rise.

I look down, "You idiot."
My hands aren't mine.

They move without me.

…"she looked into my eyes and said, 'I love you.'"

The faucet drips.
The mug tilts.
The fans twirl.

*"You're making the chances of us having an amicable
co-parenting relationship low—"*

I open my mouth,
But the sound
Is just a low bass, blurred,
Like someone speaking
Through the vents

"—Over a decade of fighting to give you a great life.
This was never supposed to be us, how did we
become this?—"

I think I logged in now—
I already did.
Or maybe
I never did.

The light shifts.
The hum stops.
The room folds
Into itself.

"—I'm tired of begging for bare minimums, for years now! I deserve better—"

I'm still alone here.
I was more alone there
At least now my loneliness makes sense.
Feeling the absence.
Again.
Again.
Again.

DEPRESSION

Each morning I reluctantly awaken
in the room at the end of the hall—
in the place they call home.
That word scrapes against me, because it doesn't fit.
Not anymore.
Not since I carried my life out of the old house
in boxes that smelled of dust and her perfume.

I take a shot of whiskey to forget that smell.

The window here faces east,
but somehow the morning light arrives tired,
filtered through the same floral curtains that hung
here when I was a teenager.
When the air still meant something clean and
possible.
Now, it just hangs in the room like stale breath,
unmoving. The air mattress is uncomfortable;
It swallows me in a slow, forgiving way that feels
cruel.

I take a shot of bourbon to forget the discomfort.

I hear someone moving downstairs,
the soft clatter of dishes, the hum of morning routines
that no longer include me.
I think about getting up,
about making small talk,

but the thought itself feels heavier than my own body.
So I stay put: half-asleep, half-remembering.
There are boxes stacked in the corner,
leftovers from my past.
Shirts that she bought, shoes I don't wear.
Everything else that resembled a memory
was introduced to the marketplace.
What remains still emits a painful kind of quiet,
a density that pulls at me,
a reminder that everything I own
had been hand-picked for a life that no longer exists.

I take a shot of moonshine to forget the past decade.

Having a dream is a rarity for me;
but when I do, sometimes I dream of the house
I bought her for her birthday,
how excited she was about all the space,
the playground, the basketball court, the gardens.
Now, those dreams all have that moment
of inescapable plummeting
and being jolted awake right before you hit the
bottom.
So I lie in one of a dozen positions,
feeling the urge to cry, but my faculties are too numb
to process the request.
Instead, I count the same shadows on the ceiling.
I take a shot of whiskey to go back to sleep.

By sunrise, I'm supposed to get up
and be a contributing member of society but—for
what? Nobody's going to wonder where I am.

The ceiling is the only unblinking witness of my
absence.
I take a shot of whiskey and toast to these four walls,
thanking them for their cold indifference to my long
nights.
The air feels like damp fabric laid over my face,
Not enough to suffocate but enough to press.
To remind me of the weight of existing
in a life that no longer recognizes me.
The light leaking through the blinds is colorless,
exhausted, as if it, too, has given up trying to mean
anything.
I take a shot of moonshine because it means
I don't have to be reminded of how much of a failure
I am.

I make it a double shot to forget
how my babies may never forgive me
for taking away "home".

There is coffee somewhere downstairs.
I remember pouring it yesterday—or was it the day
Before?—the smell of it—dark and bitter,
the cup cooling in my hand
until it became another thing I could not hold onto.
My body moves in small ways:
the slow turn of the head,
the shallow breath,
the shifting of a foot beneath the blanket.
But it feels like watching an old film reel,
the kind where the sound drags a second behind the
picture and nothing quite lines up.

I move, eventually, because time insists,
Though it feels more like gravity pulling than choice.
My legs are slow; my breath uneven;
and each step makes a quiet, thick sound against the
floor—as though the carpet itself has turned to mud.
There are moments, brief and uncertain,
when I feel the edge of myself blur.
as though I could dissolve into the dim hum of the
refrigerator, the low sigh of the house, the endless
gray between thought and nothing...
And in those moments,
I understand what it means to disappear without
dying—
to keep living inside a life that no longer fits,
wearing a name that no longer answers,
moving through a world that keeps turning,
too heavy to hold,
too empty to stop.

So I take a shot of moonshine to forget that I exist.

INSOMNIA

I find no rest, no matter how I try;
The twenty-four hours spin inside my head,
The clock torments with shadows of the camera's
cold, dilated eye.

I regret this man I forged beneath the sky,
Who became a light to keep a vampire fed—
I find no rest, no matter how I try.

I plead to the heavens, wishing I could lie
In peace, but my brain performs forensics
on the dead;
The clock torments with shadows of the camera's
cold, dilated eye.

The onslaught of oak-aged defenses runs dry,
Like a lone survivor hanging by a thread;
I find no rest, no matter how I try.

Make it stop! To the other dimension, I would fly,
Where time is still and heavy as the lead;
The clock torments with shadows of the camera's
cold, dilated eye.

Memory insists that sleep is something
spirits can supply,
I take a shot of moonshine before bed—a deceptive
lie.

I find no rest, no matter how I try.
The clock torments with shadows of the camera's
cold, dilated eye.

II. TABES [TAH • bess]

— — — — — — — — — — — — — — — — — —

THE KING

I fled the torrid throne of my bastion,

Keeping stock of the crown,

Preserved in flesh; a canvas that time can touch,

But not erase.

Where I once sipped cranberry from a royal chalice,

Now styrofoam cradles what remains of that glory—

A testament of foolish concessions—

Royal whipsaw.

While the throne no longer bears my name,

The queen still acknowledges my cold, quiet majesty;

As her voice trembles with the echo of past vows,

And she leans into the warmth of her new king.

Royal whipsaw.

"Are you resolved with ending the marriage? ...So you don't want me back? Fully?"

"You are all I have ever wanted. Fully. But now I get to watch you be that for someone else."

"I know I've said this before but you seem really happy. You're almost glowing. It sucks that I don't get to know the healed version of you."

"You have absolutely changed."

"I'm just trying to find out if it's for better or for worse. I can't tell who I am."

"You ARE A KING!!! That's who!"

"Thank you. Those words from anybody else are just words; I always needed to hear it from you."

"I'm sorry it took so long."

I stare, engrossed, at the word "King"—

Royal whipsaw.

Wearing a Jester's crown.

King of the air mattress.

King of reliving "Rushes" every night.

King of a castle built of dust.

Royal whipsaw.

It's easy to call someone a King,

When your heart no longer has to bow to him.

As if I've made enemies with the heavens,

Showering me in its cruel irony,

Her ringtone alone disturbs the always-on display—

With a faint interest in how a dethroned King endures.

A ceaseless reality check offered by the same hand

Holding the knife that nudged my crown to the floor.

She gets just close enough to see the blood,

Then retreats into the arms where her heart bows.

Her: "Can you take the kids Tuesday? I have a late shift."

This is being a King...

DRIED INK

A rapid ascent to the presumed peak,

But ignorance is a poor tour guide.

Not an expert on survival technique,

I was ill-equipped for this ride.

At the crest of denial, I looked to a stone-faced pillar,

Unbothered by the gravity of woe.

His words delivered a stone-cold shiver,

He said it plain: "I told you so."

Doused in confusion, the lesson is learned,

(I suspect no ill-intent, just reality).

"I wish I felt bad for how you've burned,

But I don't... and I say that with clarity."

His words are sharp, but the wisdom is keen,

The voice that warned of the delusion inside.

The eyes that watched as I made a scene,

And bartered my senses away for pride.

The voice that tried to stop the transgression,

Before I made my "Foolish Concessions."

Unable to process, it just feels mean,

Probing for clarity on what is real.

I abruptly pause on the ruins' routine—

Convinced my self-made wound will never heal.

Time has aged; no more discussions.

Isolation is the cost of my survival.

His voice remains the whip's repercussion,

While we wait for friendship's revival.

For now, what I've birthed, I hold close—

All while knowing the ink dried just as he wrote.

HEARTS IN HALF-LIGHT

There is a hush beneath my grin: a weightless void,

Creeping within as I wear the night with no name.

A silent guest who speaks in flame.

If love is a healer, its ghosts must be necrosis.

Hunting for first aid in the skin of strangers.

I swipe… we match… we meet. The geometry of the chase.

"*There's a lot we like about you, but…*"

The collective verdict hangs, dressed in polite concern,

A cruel pattern, orchestrated by the past.

I can't care enough to alter the verdict.

My heart exists in a coma; my body roams.

I seek that soft voice of reassurance—Silence.

It's where I fill in the blanks with leftover maelstrom.

Text message interviews and Facetime confirmations,

All to prove the existence of a new ghost—"Read"

The thread is tied to an eerie quiet.

My past keeps whispering its autopsy.

I came for your eyes, not to retrace the ruins—

There's a body beneath all that history.

The doctors severed the future

to save a past that left.

They put a period where my lineage stops.

I am a dead end for love seeking a new Aedes.

I'll never fit the full family portrait.

Every date feels like a test

of how gently I can break a dream.

The half of my heart that is hidden from the light

Is the ugliest part: dressed in scar tissue and stitches.

Burdened by the weight of a glacier,

Trudging through mistrust,

Begging for a warm breath to melt it all away.

THE QUIET BEFORE THE MEMO

In sequence, my depression—a voracious mouth—

Satiated by the carcass of what was my life.

Blank days in the office, with unblinking eyes.

The inbox groans with yet another meeting,

This one carrying "URGENT" in the subject line.

A sensation arrives—

I recognize the symptoms, but the ache is numb

I take a shot of whiskey to keep it that way

I dial in, screened by equanimity.

   "...We noticed your numbers are down this quarter..."

My shadow watches with a silent smirk,

As the hunter becomes the prey.

But my face has forgotten the shape of a smile.

"We want to make sure you are aligned with what the business demands. How are things? Are you okay?"

I force the words away from my lips:

"I'm just tired, bone-deep tired.

I can't sleep,

I haven't eaten in days;

I can't focus, I—"

He interjects while nodding, *"Well, HR asked me to discuss your performance with you..."*

My lungs went still... my face a neutral mask...

Hiding the war behind my eyes—

My demons, my kids, now my job.

He continues...

"...we understand external stressors...missed deadlines...

incomplete deliverables..."

My eyelids feel like rusted gates.

I'm ascending—

Watching this interaction from the ceiling.

I climb back into my body and ask him to repeat

I told him my connection dropped.

"Is there something affecting your ability to perform? This is uncharacteristic of you..."

I kindly offer a one-word gift: "Divorce."

"Ooooohhh...why didn't you say anything sooner?"

I figured I'd own the fault like all else,

And not present the cause—

However valid the plea.

"We believe you can get back on track... We'll follow up with a plan and hope to see progress in 30 days."

A phantom panic, just beyond the reach of my tongue.

I saw his mouth moving but his words fell right through me.

I sat for hours with the wall—a companion.

Blank watching blank.

Only one of us belittled.

Who's failing the audit now?

SOMATIC

This life is a gym membership—

    with a cancellation policy

        designed to

            fail.

Quick workouts

            turn into life lessons,

treadmill miles spiraling me into

    confusion and

            hopelessness.

Bench-pressing the weight of the world,

    feeling invincible

          for a minute

until the bar sinks—

    too heavy—

        and there's

no one

                                  spotting me.

My memory—wait what was I saying—

      My life loops back

  full circle

          to the squat rack.

Day after day,

       plate after plate,

          rep after rep,

              ache after ache—

          and then

      the body

starts

  giving up

with me.

My memory—a blank wall

where the story stood.

                Legs no longer willing

to bend at the knee,

every angle accompanied by

crackling ligaments,

popping joints—

(a Morse Code of failure).

Doctors say

severe stress can trigger arthritis.

They say it's why the right side

of my body goes

numb

(numb)

(n u m b).

Even better—

It's rheumatoid.

The ache each time I breathe,

the tightness across the chest—

that's anxiety.

The battle to get out of bed—

that's
depression.

The ten-second attention span—

ADHD crashing the party

while PTSD holds the door.

The "D" stands for
Disorder

(I always read it as Dissociation)—

my brain shielding me

from the trauma

it still remembers.

Probably why

I can't dream

(or won't).

Can't sleep either—

and you have to be asleep

to dream...

kind of.

I'm starting to look

as sick

as I imagine

I'm supposed to feel—

twenty pounds vanished

while my appetite and sleep

did the same.

Doctor says my liver is begging for mercy,

enzymes shooting

through the roof—

Imagine trying to beat
depression

with a depressant.

Genius.

Each buzz of the phone—

rollercoaster drop,

thinking someone thought of me

but it's just
an email.

Always

a

damn

email.

And then—

I passed out

in the street,

probably from

...everything.

I'm quitting.

My body's quitting.

And

I'm...

B

L

A

N

K.

III. INTERITUS [in • tuh • REE • toos]

INTERITUS FRACTUS

B

   L

A

   N

K

What light—

   What brilliance blinds me to everything but darkness?

"She doesn't want you, stupid!"

     "You failed! You fucking lose! AGAIN!"

Time is a god that offers no refunds.

     "You thought you were important? Pfft..."

"Now he's hugging your babies!"

13 YEARS—

What my body spent and my spirit endured.

"You lose! You fucking loser!"

The cost carved in effort and grief.

"Why don't you want me?"

I tried—

and tried—

IT WAS NEVER ENOUGH! FU—

IT WAS NEVER GOING TO BE ENOUGH!!!

"Pssst...hey..."

"Mr. Wesson made something for times like this..."

A lucid instant cutting through the haze,

"Even she said sometimes she wishes you'd married someone else JACKASS!"

A scale to show me the gravity of my commitment

From the deepest place inside, fear roars...

"I failed my babies, I took their home"

I shudder; I send out a cryptic SOS—radio silence...

A sense of urgency trembles my fingers,

"*Just wait 'til your babies get a new brother*"

I reach out again—radio silence...

"*Yeah, nobody cares about your pain dummy!*"

"*She doesn't care! They don't care! You don't even care anymore...*"

My eyes carry my hands toward purpose—

the curing palmswell.

Tap...

Tap...

tap...

The inferno blazing at my temple

welcomes the smooth, cold steel.

"not like that idiot!"

I know—

My tongue—unswayed by the taste of steel;

a temporary stillness; palms emptied of their darkness

"Your babies only tolerate you too!"

Sledgehammer tremors thumping my chest,

ears abuzz,

"do it..."

I listen to the whispered voice within

Grab...

Squeeze...

Click...

B

L

A

N

K

"HEY STUPID, PUSH THE CLIP ALL THE WAY IN!"

I can't even quit the right way—

(sigh)

I need a drink...

BREATHE

MORS NEGATA

Darkness has devoured

    the whole of me—

    and the sky in tandem

        I find no rest, no matter how I try;

The clock torments with shadows

    of the camera's cold, dilated eye.

A nightfall adorned in stunning rarity

          a nightmare minutely
      woven

    into my unraveling—jolted

...cold sweats

"What time is it?"—"Rushes"

    *"YOU **CAN'T** ESCAPE BY OPENING YOUR EYES..."*

I speak to the darkness, "Well I can't escape by closing them either."

    ...unless....

"YOU'LL
NEVER *BE—"*

"STOP!"

...sitting at the edge of the bed

...banging on my head, as if the voices

would come spilling out of my ears...

"Make it stop!"—my tears plead with me.

"Take a deep breath."

*"**NOBODY** WILL WANT YOU NOW. ACCEPT IT, KING!"*

I reach for my whiskey—

sobbing...feels like a hostage situation

and my tears are being freed as demands are being met

*"GUESS YOU STILL AREN'T COOL **ENOUGH**—*

STILL SINGING THAT SAME REFRAIN DECADES LATER."

"GO AHEAD. CALL HER. SEE WHO ANSWERS."

"Make it stop…"

*"EVEN YOUR BODY HAS HAD **ENOUGH** OF YOU!"*

I take the posture of beginning, and of breaking…

feeling the hair on my legs—

*"YOU BEFRIENDED MORE SKILLFUL TREACHERY. GUESS YOUR **MAELSTROM** STILL NEEDS REFINING!"*

feeling my breath on my knees

trying to inhabit a reality that doesn't drift

"Make it stop…"

*"YOUR JOB DOESN'T **CARE**; JUST FOCUS ON THE NEXT PROJECT."*

"Make it stop…"

*"HE TOLD YOU SO, **STUPID**! NOW LOOK AT YOU!"*

*"NOBODY UNDERSTANDS YOUR HEART—YOUR **LOVE**."*

"Make it stop..."

I've taken my whiskey to silence—

I reach for what's left in the bottle beside it—

"Make it stop..."

I reach for whatever is in the bottle beside—

...pills...

I let them descend into my hollowed self

each one like a small promise...

one...three...

"Make it stop..."

The clock torments with shadows...

tick... tok... tick...
tok... 4A.M.

"Make it stop..."

nine...

*"NOW YOU GET IT! YOU **DON'T** MATTER!"*

*"YOU ARE ONLY THE CAUSE OF MY **MOMENT**."*

...eleven...

Like a gentle hand upon my shoulder—serenity.

...I think I'm
almost....

"KEEP GOING"

"Make it stop..."

sixteen... ninete—

Finally...

I found—

what I hoped

would be

an eternal blink...

BREATHE

VERITAS ACCEPTA [Truth Accepted]

Beneath my eyelids—

I can feel my eyes combing the dark

Searching for truth it can't yet see

My body—a tired weight pressing into the mattress

Slow deep breaths fan a quiet heat across my face

I can feel...

My eternal blink, compressed into fleeting hours

The "Mors"(death)...

was "Negata"(denied)...

I have lost the battle to love,

My mind's fortress demolished to dust—

And death stands at the gate, unyielding.

My trophy for these monumental losses—breath

No lighter than the wreckage I transport—

A prize that mocks the doors it opens.

To stare into the mirror once more.

To quiet the maelstrom clawing inside.

To reclaim what can be mended...

Perhaps I'm failing at what I was never meant to master,

Yet, succeeding where I gave no effort.

Maybe "Mr. Maelstrom" is a suitable moniker.

But I can admit, I can't win this battle alone,

Nor can I seem to lose it alone,

I need help.

I reached for a lifeline, not just a phone...

　　　"Hi, this is Ryan, your mental health support professional..."

It's time to see if I'll succeed at being a patient.

ITER RECUPERATIONIS [Recovery Journey]

I. The Intake

Now I dwell in a room untouched,

Tasting the rawness of the world,

As I bite reality and chew shards of disgust—

Silence thundering.

"Knock, knock. It's time to take your meds."

I approach a desk displaying a chemist's riddle—

Each puzzle bearing a promise.

"The therapist will see you now."

I approach a small office—

Air thick with the scent of old wounds.

My soul in a cup—poured onto cold rocks.

I spilled it into her lap and chased it with salt rivers of grief.

The session dissipates but emotion remains.

I pour the rest of myself into a room that listens too well.

My hand bleeds and hurts—

turning pain into verse.

In this empty room.

II. The Journey

Now I live life by the hour—

Digging up bones at every intersection.

"What are you grateful for?"

"Tell me one thing you love about yourself..."

Questions that felt like a ploy at first,

Until I realized I didn't have an answer—

"What's your personality type?"

"What's your attachment style?"

"What's your love language?"

"How do you handle guilt or shame?"

172

All words clandestine while I search for an answer—

I was heavy with something I had no name for—

Repetition—a familiar rhythm

Where I uncovered a self I hadn't met:

The Fearful-Avoidant, with a deep dread of feeling.

I reach for love like I am starved—

Yet, I flinch from it,

Unconvinced I belong to it, to feel it fully anymore.

In an anonymous place, I learned—

Sobriety has a vast wardrobe—

Sometimes rough, sometimes radiant,

"Emotional Sobriety" was the outfit I hadn't seen

My drinking was never a romance My Employee:

I loved the escape—

The borrowed silence; the distance from emotion;

The distance from the rawness of being human.

As I write this, atop My Employee's resignation letter,

Seven sober months sit in my mailbox.

The would-be monarch escorted from his borrowed throne

Amidst the return of the CEO.

When you read this, I hope the count has multiplied…

My quiet testament to staying.

III. Re-emergence

A trek through the ashes of recent ruin.

The walls, the pillows, the carpet, stand in awe

Of my re-emergence alongside family.

I purged my stockpile of spirits.

Proximity won't undermine.

I meander through familiar places with unfamiliar clarity—

Watching the world move on; my return unbeknownst,

Hands still trembling from the work of rebuilding myself.

There is no parade, no crowd to greet me—

Just the soft, steady truth: I am here again,

Holding on to my trophy—

Learning how to belong in the world I once ran from.

IV. Love's Reckoning

Have you ever watched beauty arrive,

As if it carried its own light?

Even with eyes that have failed me for years—

I could see that she was blessed.

Her smile was art,

Her curves: placed exactly where imagination belongs

And the moment I saw her,

I knew I'd have to dance in the fire,

To prove I wasn't made of paper—

But nobody warned me that insecurities are highly flammable.

I felt the heat in all its glory;

Then I quickly realized, nobody is coming to save me.

She stood in a fire of her own

While I offered my scars like stepping stones—

A path into a new life. We spoke of forever,

But she chose friendship over foundation.

And I stood in the ruins of almost-love,

Empty-handed,

With a heart still learning to hold itself.

IN BIVIO [Crossroads]

Now I stand, fire-forged, charred and broken,

Starved of the spice of true love's feast.

Why invite love again?

Because the flavorless safety of loneliness

Is a taste I'm done pretending to savor.

I'm reminded that this safety is a ration, not a meal.

It keeps me from starving, but will never make me full.

But why love what you will lose?

Because nothing is forever.

And yet, a feast that ends

Is better than a famine that doesn't.

I am worthy of being loved.

Not for a week, not for a few months.

But for a lifetime...

The no good man, solo—no clan,

I'll be the storm you can't withstand,

The one you desire, but cannot command.

So stop looking for the softness in my eyes,

It's buried deep down under hard goodbyes.

That good man fought, that good man fell,

And like a Phoenix rising,

Built this fortress from hell.

So don't go trying to fix me, save your breath,

You're looking at a man...living his death...

ACKNOWLEDGEMENTS

To the blaze that redefined where I begin...thank you.

To the riot of silence that became my companion...thank you.

To those whose stride was set against my own...thank you.

To love—

To the one reading this—sifting through these ashes with me...

THANK YOU

"A gesture of grace, rising from the ruin"

ABOUT THE AUTHOR

—MISTER X—

He writes for the silent majority who are grieving a life they thought was permanent. He chronicles the journey from loss to love and back to loss so that others might recognize their own story in his. He is a voice for the invisible battles of mental health, and the visible struggles of sobriety. He writes to prove that while the ruin is personal, the experience is non-exclusive.

Instagram: @mister.x.clusive

You have sifted through the ashes.

Now, we look beneath the skin.

T H E—X—R A Y

AN INTROSPECTIVE COLLECTION

COMING SOON

Join the silent majority.

Get notified when "The—X—Ray" is exposed.

www.ingramcontent.com/pod-product-compliance
Lightning Source LLC
Chambersburg PA
CBHW060420130626
46555CB00005B/2154